Pragmatic Wisdom Vol. 4

Stoic Lessons on Learning (Teachers and Students)

James Bellerjeau

A Fine Idea

Copyright © 2025 by James Bellerjeau

All rights reserved.

No portion of this book may be reproduced in any form without written permission from the publisher or author, except as permitted by U.S. copyright law.

Contents

1. Why Do Anything? An Introduction to the Stoic Lessons — 1
2. On the Stealth Philosopher — 3
3. On Sharing Wisdom — 7
4. On True and False Philosophy — 11
5. On Easy Lessons — 15
6. On Instagram-Worthy Quotes — 21
7. On a Good Talk — 25
8. On Drinking Deeply — 29
9. On Words and Meaning — 33
10. On Your New Blog — 39
11. On Good Examples — 43
12. On Continuing Education — 45
13. On the Best Course of Study — 51
14. On How To Study Philosophy — 59
15. On Precepts (Sayings) — 65

16. On a Learning Mind   73

17. On New Students   81

Chapter One

Why Do Anything? An Introduction to the Stoic Lessons

Dear friends. Join me on a journey to discover what it means to live a good life. Our inspiration in this quest is Seneca's Moral Letters to Lucilius, revisited and revised for our modern times. The search for what it means to live a good life was not new in Seneca's day, and it will not be old when we are all long gone.

Although these are not Seneca's letters, they honor both his wisdom and his instructions for new students. That is, we should grapple with deep thoughts and make our understanding of the truth personal.

Because no one has a monopoly on the truth, we can each contribute to the puzzle. **The reason to do anything is to answer a question that has not been answered, or at a minimum to answer it for yourself.**

In answering life's deepest questions, would it not be foolish for us to pass by the foundational stones laid by the great thinkers who labored before us? Seneca himself in search of inspiration says in his Letter 2:

> I am wont to cross over even into the enemy's camp, — not as a deserter, but as a scout.

Let us all be avid scouts of the great thinkers, seeking out their every camp with the mindset of anthropologists unearthing meaning from among the ruins. Although Seneca's words have been mined by many for centuries, each generation keeps turning up gemstones.

Thus, with this series of Pragmatic Wisdom for Busy People, let us polish old stones to show them in a new light, and in washing off the mud and debris, reveal what fresh reflections may appear.

Be well.

PS — You can read each of the volumes independently, as it suits your time and your interests. Dedicated readers will find, however, that their understanding of each volume will increase upon reading further volumes. The sincere student may therefore wish to have the full set of Stoic letters: Pragmatic Wisdom for the Sincere Student.

Chapter Two

On the Stealth Philosopher

Nothing turns a sharp ear deaf more quickly than the listener sensing you feel superior to them

G reetings dear reader!

I take heart in the fact that you are daily working to improve yourself. The path to greatness is not traveled in one giant leap. It is the accumulation of many miles that require a lifetime of walking.

But although the journey is a thousand miles, your task each day is the same: Make sure you take at least a single step.

Do not let your progress go to your head, however, and by no means should you preen your development before your fellow travelers. Nothing turns a sharp ear deaf more quickly than the listener sensing you feel superior to them.

Perhaps you have heard the phrase "pacing and leading" and wondered what it meant. It's simply this. If you mean to influence another to change, you first must come into harmony with them: I hear your words, I understand your situation, I feel your pain.

It is not just on the mental plane that you seek to harmonize. You may breach the gates of their resistance by observing and subtly adopting the posture, emotions, and mannerisms of your audience. It is only when the gates have been unlocked, let alone flung open, that your words can find entry.

Once the resistance of your audience's minds has been loosened by your pacing, then, and only then, do you have a chance to lead.

You lead by *showing* the way, and not by *forcing* anyone along the path. The moment your pupils feel pushed, they will rear up like stubborn donkeys and go no further. He treads the path most surely when it is a path of his own choosing.

Numerous other ways in which you may spook the horse: Either through an overly aggressive delivery or a manner of dress inconsistent with your message.

Just as we would buy no suit from a disheveled tailor, take fitness lessons from an unfit instructor, or follow the health advice of a smoking doctor, so will your audience dismiss even your brightest observations if you deliver them from an inappropriate vessel. If you wish your fine wine to be enjoyed to the fullest, serve it from a crystal decanter.

Although we struggle to discern others' true intentions and inner thoughts, we have no such difficulty judging their appearance. True, appearance is irrelevant to the truth of your words, but for your words to work, you first must be heard.

Nor should you make the opposite mistake of dressing yourself too ornately, for this too will strike your audience falsely. If your audience is one that is comfortable in jeans, why then so must you be if you hope to have them hear you.

And if to another group casual Friday means not wearing the pin-striped vests of their three-piece suits, then you may break out your suit and tie. Know your audience first by fitting in with them, and they will know the truth of your words.

Here for your daily improvement is an idea that will give you companionship on many a quiet night's contemplation. The Buddha advises us to let go of both grasping and aversion.

- Cease to desire, and your monkey mind will be calmed.
- Cease to push away things you dislike, and likewise, you will calm your troubled spirit.

"But how," you ask, "can avoiding two polar opposites create the same effect?"

In this way, my dear reader: Though they seem like opposites, they are in fact the same. Just as gravity causes the feather and the cannonball to fall at the same rate, so grasping and aversion both find the same cause in our fear.

In the case of grasping, we fear not getting what we desire (or losing that which we have acquired). In the case of aversion, we fear being confronted with that which is hateful or painful.

The fear is rooted in another cause, namely not centering your mind in the present. It is only in the future that we may lose what we currently possess or be harmed by that which may afflict us.

To be able to see into the future the consequences of our actions is humankind's greatest advantage. But this foresight comes at the cost of carrying back haunts and demons that bedevil us.

Banish worries about tomorrow to where they belong — the future! They have no place in your daily meditation.

Be well.

Chapter Three

On Sharing Wisdom

Wisdom shared is wisdom doubled, and nothing pleases me more than adding to the store of wisdom in the world

G reetings!

I feel, dear reader, that I am not only continuously improving, but have become improved.

I do not yet, however, fool myself with the fantasy that I need no further refinement. There are many among us who could benefit from less flab or flirting with fame and firmer muscles.

That I see my own failings with fresh eyes does not depress me. I take it as a sign that my perception is sharpening. And if these thoughts are just placebos, am I not yet healthier for their consumption?

It is with this optimism that I am encouraged even further to respond to your questions. I see in you the same desire to improve, not least in your acknowledgment of doubt. I too doubted, and a problem shared is a problem halved.

How you would rejoice to know how much I feel I have come to understand, and how this wisdom grows daily. "Share this wisdom with me," I hear you already, and I tell you I do so gladly.

Wisdom shared is wisdom doubled, and nothing pleases me more than adding to the store of wisdom in the world.

If bad news is an orphan, good news has many parents. Let the truth be fruitful and multiply and let any who wish stake a claim to parentage.

You do not lack sources of truth. Thanks to the internet, the wisdom of all ages is but a keystroke away. Why then do so many fail to gain wisdom from the source that flows endlessly at their feet?

You do not understand water if you will not wade into the river. When your feet stand on pebbles smoothed by the eons of water passing over them, you may gain firsthand a feeling of the truth that a lifetime spent reading will not impart.

Saying is not enough, only doing. Reading is not enough, only doing. Do not do as I *say*, do as I *do*.

And now I both say and do thusly: Remember to follow systems, not goals. That is to say, adopt simple habits that move you in the right direction, rather than focusing on the desired destination.

If you want to lose weight, rather than setting a goal of losing ten pounds, remove the unhealthy snacks from your house and buy fruits and vegetables instead. When you are hungry and have only healthy options to hand you are more likely to choose correctly.

In this way, you increase your chances of success regardless of which shores you wanted to wash up on. Knowing where you want to go helps set a direction, true. But a direction alone brings you no closer to your goal. (You will find Scott Adams a most able teacher if you want to know more about systems versus goals.)

Many daydream of starting a business, becoming wealthy, or achieving high office. How much more useful to know what steps you need to take on your journey.

Researching these steps is not difficult, and many who have gone before you have shared their steps. Consider Cal Newport or Tim Ferris if you want a point to jump from. Taking daily steps along the path of continuous improvement will render your ultimate destination irrelevant, even as it increases your chances of arriving there.

I leave you with this small thought of the day, which gave me pleasure when thinking of you. It is this phrase from Ronald Reagan, who understood that a single step, no matter how small, will help so long as it is a step in the right direction:

> We can't help everyone, but everyone can help someone.

Be well.

Chapter Four

On True and False Philosophy

Remember that philosophy is neither just for show nor for other people's benefit

I suspect I don't need to convince you, dear reader, that the unexamined life is unlikely to be guided by wisdom.

A person may be blessed by Fortune, and to all outward appearances successful. But if they themselves do not contemplate the purpose of their existence, what separates them from well-tended beasts of burden in our fields and pastures? We can pity them as worse off than the impoverished pilgrims taking their very first steps along the path of meaning.

The more you consider the reasons for the right actions, the more enlightened you will become. And though your work takes you a lifetime, still you are better for each day's toil than those living in ignorant luxury. Their supposed happiness relies on luck alone and can be taken from them without notice.

You do not need to put on a show for me to make me understand your progress is no mere performance. And though I know your intentions are good, remember that philosophy is neither just for show nor for other people's benefit. It is personal and for you.

Philosophy is not just words but must drive your thoughts and actions. Although you may think you have learned to walk the path, be careful that in your confidence you do not raise your eyes to the horizon and thus lose your way. Just as your feet must stay grounded, so too should your thoughts.

A well-ordered mind is at constant risk of being thrown out of equilibrium. Each day brings countless opportunities to test your foundation. If any test is not met with success, whether through the failure of resolve or through simple inattention, you give up ground previously hard-won.

Your opponents peddling alternative philosophies are many and will include the physicist, the deist, and the atheist.

- The physicist tells you that "Everything that is and will be is determined by fixed rules that govern the interaction of all particles. Show me the matter existing a moment after the Big Bang, and I will tell you the action of every atom for eternity."

- The deist cries "Nonsense! All we are and will be is in God's hands, and only God determines the fate of the Universe and all its beings."

- And quietly the atheist is heard to mutter, "There is no god, there are no universal rules, there is only now, and I am not sure what that means."

ON TRUE AND FALSE PHILOSOPHY

I ask you dear reader, what meaning exists in a collision of quarks and gluons? Should meaning be found in surrendering intellect to blind faith?

Whether the future is foreordained or in the hands of an all-powerful referee, or rather we are careening along in a game of chance, only philosophy provides a framework to give our lives meaning.

And though some or all hypotheses may hold portions of the true nature of reality, we are all still bound to the mortal plain. Thus, the more we draw our attention away from the invisible, whether vast or tiny and focus the locus of control on ourselves and our thoughts, the closer we can come to a meaningful life.

In case your mind has wandered in search of what additional treasure my letter holds, you need stray no further. For I have been to China on your behalf and have brought back this gem from Lao Tzu:

> Be content with what you have, rejoice in the way things are. When you realize there is nothing lacking, the whole world belongs to you.

Consider the differences between true desires (those consistent with nature) and false desires (those going against nature).

- True desires originate within you and are satisfied within you.

- False desires originate externally, and your attempts to satisfy them are external to you.

You are hungry, you eat, and your body signals when you are satiated, provided you are listening. You exercise your muscles, you burn energy and your muscles tire, and you will stop when you have had enough. These are true desires.

Contrast now the desire for money or fame or possessions. How many do you know who, upon gaining a million dollars, did not find their appetite whetted for even more? Having lined up an imposing line of zeros, there is always room for one more.

And the seeker of fame is never satisfied, for there is always another who has more followers, more likes, and simply more. When you look to external things for your happiness, each purchase offers but a crumb against your insatiable hunger.

You can one-click order until your cart is filled to overflowing, but you will hollow yourself out trying to fill a bottomless chasm.

The British philosopher Bertrand Russell understood the difference between true and false philosophy. He stated it thusly:

> It is preoccupation with possessions, more than anything else, that prevents men from living freely and nobly.

Be well.

Chapter Five

On Easy Lessons

Everywhere we turn, we are confronted with the incredible shrinking attention span

You have mentioned to me twice now that the study of philosophy is out of vogue for most people, and that the written word is so antique as to be virtually forgotten.

If we are not on Facebook, X, or Instagram, or better yet posting a weekly Spotify podcast or YouTube video, then we might as well put on our orthopedic shoes and sweater vest and spend the afternoons playing Bingo at the senior home.

Everywhere we turn, we are confronted with the incredible shrinking attention span.

- Who has the time to read entire books when Blinkist can give you the gist in a blink?

- Why watch a movie in a theater when you can stream 30-minute episodes on any device wherever you are?

- And who has thirty minutes to watch a full episode, when fifteen-second diversions are available nonstop at the flick of a finger?

You can scarcely finish a thought before the mind has wandered, flitting about like a hummingbird on the non-stop search for nectar.

"In such an environment," you say, "surely it is folly to expect to find an attentive audience willing to sit and do the hard work of reading and thinking. Hadn't we best adapt our message for the audience's abilities?"

It's true, we could chew our message to cud and spit it out for a slack-jawed crowd to mindlessly slurp. Though we would surely extend our reach to the broadest audience in this way, my dear reader, we would also dilute our message until it lost its meaning.

Do you teach an athlete to run a marathon by strolling around the block? Or to lift a great weight by putting feathers on one's forearms? No, and nor do we train the mind when we give it such light fare.

Little effort means little progress. It is ruminating on deep thoughts that generates growth, not consuming half-digested musings.

I don't suppose the glitterati will let this challenge go unanswered. They will pile up the charges against us and make the case thusly: "If you can't express your ideas simply in ways an average person can understand, you don't understand them yourself."

This we may hear from a Hollywood starlet whose claim to fame is a nub nose and a symmetrical face that is as much the result of gifted plastic surgery as genetics. I can see why they prefer the simpleton's version, but the arrows they shoot at us never hit their mark, because they cannot hit what they do not know to aim at.

Our critics do not surrender, but rather they turn their weapons on our audience: "The Stoics' medicine is bitter, and their course of recovery long and hard. Come to our side, and we will make everything easy for you: The one-hour workday, the no-discipline diet, and the no-sacrifice path to success!"

This is appealing fare, no doubt, and it will attract the masses as surely as it fails to nourish them. The only guarantee the consumer of such light sustenance can be sure of is that another snack will be available for purchase just as soon as this one disappears from your monthly credit card statement.

Deep down, do we not know when we are being sold nostrums and snake oil? We are willing dupes in being dazzled by packaging and bamboozled by dust-jacked blurbs. Show me a popular self-help author, and I will show you someone who has chosen to sell surface appeal instead of depth, and platitudes over purpose.

The greater the renown among the public, the less likely you are to have served before you gourmet food. For the masses want cheap and tasty meals, and you deliver these in quantity by following mass-production principles.

There is one type of reading that I give you my blessing, indeed my urging, to avoid at all costs: That is self-help books of almost any kind.

"What?" you wonder. "Am I to discard the advice of experts altogether? And how ironic that you who are so keen on dispensing wisdom forbid my seeking it from others."

What we are discussing in these letters, my dear reader, are truths and wisdom that belong to no expert, but are the common good of mankind. Furthermore, we are picking them up not as finished goods but must adapt, amend, and apply our lessons in a personal context.

Your self-help expert generally comes in two flavors: The scholar who has studied tables of figures until they tease or torture out statistical significance, and the business executive who explains their success in hindsight and with a healthy dose of selective memory.

As to the first, whether squeezed between unprovable hypotheses and the repeatability crisis, you are likely as well served by consulting your palm reader as you are the academic under pressure to publish.

And as to expecting the average executive to have sufficient self-reflection to understand the role factors beyond luck played in their fortune, let's just say you will get as useful advice from the one who explains how they picked the numbers for the winning lottery ticket.

In freeing you of this burden, I have greatly eased your load, for there are now whole aisles in the bookstore you may profitably avoid. In return, I ask you to stop and consider this:

> Whenever you find yourself on the side of the majority, it is time to pause and reflect.

The majority are often not wrong, of course, but they are not right just by virtue of being many.

"What philosopher uttered these words?" you ask.

It was the American humorist and fantabulist Mark Twain. Having long catered to the masses in aid of keeping his coffers stocked, the man also known as Samuel Clemens in his private time knew well this lesson: That to reach the greatest audience you must appeal to the least common denominator.

Better that we count our students on one hand than sell out our principles for profit.

Be well.

Chapter Six

On Instagram-Worthy Quotes

You mustn't take the headline for the whole of the message but rather read on

What has become of my closing quotes, you wonder, where I shared wisdom collected from sages across the ages. Am I no longer able to reinforce each letter with the lessons duly noted from earlier masters?

Fear not, my store of pithy sayings has not been depleted.

The Stoics alone numbered many who became adept at condensing their knowledge into rich kernels, making them easy to pass on and share. One sees their influence across the intervening centuries, in students as diverse as Shakespeare, C.S. Lewis, and Steve Jobs.

The Stoics, in turn, represent but a fraction of notable thinkers who have grappled with great truths. Thus, from sources without end, we have a rich menu of maxims to choose from.

Moreover, for any single idea, you can call upon ten or twenty formulations, each of which either reiterates or reformulates a central theme.

The sayings we collect and repeat do serve laudable purposes: They whet our appetites to know more, they refresh our memory of what we have already studied, and they provide a glimpse through an opened window of what truths lie beyond.

But just as the container is not the content, the maxim is not the full message, only a key for interpreting the map. Though one may memorize a thousand sayings, and repeat them back in any setting, are they any better than a trained parrot?

A chatbot may respond to any of a hundred programmed questions, but are you having a meaningful interaction? Alexa on your countertop has become your daily conversationalist, but if you probe beneath the surface will you find anything of substance?

Thus, I caution you, my dear reader, that to know why an idea is worthy of study at all, you need to digest more than Instagram-worthy morsels. Such light fare may be eagerly sought by the masses, but not the sincere student.

You mustn't take the headline for the whole of the message but rather read on. Read widely and deeply.

I want you to walk the grounds that gave root to an idea, wallow in the soil that nourished it, and be drenched by the summer storms that gave it strength. If you tend to the garden of ideas

ON INSTAGRAM-WORTHY QUOTES

in this way, you will know not only how the fruits there came to ripen, but you will enjoy an abundant harvest.

Now consider this: No matter how strong the seed stock you start with, would you be a mere tender of another's crop, or will you add something new to the storehouse of humankind's bounty?

When you are the master of your garden, you can cross-pollinate ideas and bring whole new lineages of thought into being.

I think that although you may start out with what others thought, you need to end up with what you think.

Be well.

Chapter Seven

On a Good Talk

Give me persons of any age who have made their own choice to learn, not because anyone compels them to, but because they believe it will bring them something of value

If there is a better way to communicate with another person than by face-to-face conversation, I do not know it.

Our letters are certainly valuable, for when I write to you I picture you in my mind and it is as if I am speaking with you directly. And a letter from you is a bright spot in my day, in which I feel like I can hear the voice of an old friend.

What then should we think of the various ways in which today's teacher reaches out to pupils?

At one end we have the MOOC, or massive open online course. Any can join (open), and thousands do (massive), and all interactions take place remotely (online). One great voice can reach the masses, and I suppose we can be thankful for the democratization of learning.

But though each has supposed access to the master, I expect only a fraction feel truly addressed, because they are being talked *at* not talked *to*. As a result, while many begin such courses, few complete them. Have we really brought learning to the masses, or only given them a glimpse but left them wanting?

If the MOOC suffers from students lacking commitment, should we expect a better outcome when we apply a selection process? That is when we admit only students who have met some sort of qualification?

This may increase the chance that our words will land on attentive ears, but I am not yet satisfied.

- Consider how many students are present out of obligation rather than thirst for knowledge.

- They were compelled to complete their grade school, though they would have preferred to do anything but learn.

- Many are similarly prodded along to college because they are told they need a degree for success in life.

Do these children any more willingly roll from their beds, shoulder their backpacks, and fill morning lecture halls?

Give me persons of any age who have made their own choice to learn, not because anyone compels them to, but because they believe it will bring them something of value.

With such students, we can talk. Not talk at, or even talk to, but talk *with*. The best lecturer does not just lecture but also listens.

ON A GOOD TALK

The best class is one in which the professor learns something from the students, all while the students are learning. It is hard, it is rare, and it is special when it happens.

The larger the group, the greater the inhibition on speaking one's mind. This is because we fear looking foolish more than we fear remaining ignorant.

Have you noticed how often a large group will sit in silence until one brave soul says they do not understand? Suddenly there is a chorus of voices affirming, "I have the same question!"

Treat each interaction, my dear reader, whether with five, with twenty, or with a multitude, as a conversation with a single earnest person, and you have a chance of being understood by all.

Be well.

Chapter Eight

On Drinking Deeply

Think of a summary as but a sip, nourishing if it comes after a full meal, but leaving you empty if you have consumed nothing before it

You have requested that I outline for you the main teachings of philosophy that we are discussing, and I am happy to do so. A summary of key points is surely useful if it is in the hands of one who has intimate experience with what is being summarized.

But what of the one who wishes merely to memorize the list, and confuses the aphorism for the underlying wisdom?

A nail is useful to hold two pieces of wood together and fix a point between them. But if your toolbox is filled only with nails, you will be an impoverished carpenter.

Better the one who knows why this piece of wood and not another, why this length, and how these beams support the weight of the structure. And better still the one who can tell you what it is that they are building.

If you would be a capable builder, you must learn the complete skills of the trade. It is not enough to strap on the toolbelt, because all this does is put you in proximity to dangerous implements.

We do not let lawyers loose with but a book of quotes or give doctors access to our bodies if they've had access to no more than a season of Dr. House.

Serious work requires serious study, and a summary is best in the hands of the accomplished student and not the novice. Think of a summary as but a sip, nourishing if it comes after a full meal, but leaving you empty if you have consumed nothing before it.

You are an accomplished student, dear reader, because you are comfortable drawing directly from the sources of wisdom. When you read the writing of the great philosophers who have labored for our benefit before us, you are drinking deeply from wells that never run dry.

You also know that by slowing down your pace, you advance your progress. Rather than flitting from one thought to the next like a bee on an endless hunt for pollen, you can dwell in one place until your needs are met.

To know the difference between needs and wants is to start to bend your will to obtain the one and avoid the other. What most people seek most avidly, you avoid assiduously.

The greatest risk is getting what you want too quickly. If you are met with early success, in your studies, in your career, or in relationships, you have no cause to question what you are doing.

The established path — finish your studies, earn money to care for yourself and loved ones, and strive to be a person worthy of love and respect — exists for a reason, and you do not better yourself by being contrarian for the sake of it.

But nor should you blindly accept the fare put in front of you. Taste what is on offer and decide for yourself which parts are to your liking.

Know that what you consume daily will become your habit, and left unobserved your habit will become your vice.

Many take pleasure not only in the vice itself but in surrendering to the vice. Surrendering means you have made your decision and no longer need to think about what you want, but only to pursue it.

And because thinking for oneself is the hardest thing, it is no surprise that so many wish to be done with it as soon as possible.

But to give in to wants because it is easy is to expose yourself to a life of hardship. If losing access to a vice will make you sad or mad, you are mad not to cut it from your life.

I say excise the want, not the thing. You can still enjoy all that you eat and drink and have, so long as you will not miss them when you do not have them.

Always observe what you are doing and ensure that you are doing it of your own choosing. In this way, your habits become the summary of your prior deep thinking and not evidence of your absence of thought.

Be well.

Chapter Nine

On Words and Meaning

A gifted thinker turns words into more than words by adding meaning. This particular alchemy comes about when we go beyond the surface and address what is of lasting value

You say that you are overwhelmed by the number of books there are to read. Your bookshelves are overflowing, your Kindle is full, and there are not enough hours in the day to read a fraction of the homework you've assigned to yourself.

Do not assume that reading more titles will deepen your understanding of more subjects. And do not think that reading faster will hasten your progress to any destination other than confusion.

The more a person brags about being widely read, the greater the chances they are a shallow thinker. When you flit from one book to the next, sampling great writers across time, you pick up fleeting impressions of the places you visit, no more.

If you want to get a true sense of a city, you must linger in its streets, mingle with its citizens, and match your pace to its rhythms. Better you spend a month in one place than you book a whirlwind tour with twenty stops.

"I understand," you say, "and I would rather you gave me your thoughts directly than shorten my reading list."

Nothing would give me greater pleasure, my dear reader, than to see you again and have this conversation in person. The social distancing of the pandemic era may have kept us healthy in body, but the isolation is making us ill in spirit.

The Zoom meeting and Teams call are but thin comfort compared to the hearty embrace of a hale companion. I yearn for the day when I can add my vaccine passport to my traveling kit and once more point my boots on the road in your direction.

Until then, you ask me to send you my thoughts in the next best form, these letters. I do not flatter myself that you prefer my words to those of the bestsellers scattered around you because you think I am creating great fare.

But compared to wilted greens, day-old bread, and thin gruel, any meal prepared freshly will seem fine.

I would have you think of me not as the master of the kitchen, but as a dedicated sous chef: learned but still learning, always ready for a lesson from the greats.

What every great cook knows is that they do not own the secret to good taste. Everyone who puts a knife to the cutting board is entitled to experiment and improve.

But let us make sure we spend time on substantive improvements. I may probe and explore a topic from all sides, but I do not fool myself that I am describing ten different things when I am using ten different words.

A pinch of salt, a dash of pepper, a sprig of parsley: The seasoning does not make a new dish. This is one of the risks with sayings, and why I have cautioned you not to mistake the summary for the full idea.

The saying should call up in your mind a chorus of voices, each containing a few notes and bars of the larger composition. Just as the printed recipe is far from the finished meal, the saying is but an index entry, pointing to the page where the recipe is described in detail.

And though you may know what steps to follow, you must still collect the ingredients and perform your transformation upon them.

What separates the gifted chef from the uninspired is not the components they start with. Give two cooks equal amounts of rice, beans, herbs, and butter, and be amazed at how varied the results will be.

A gifted thinker turns words into more than words by adding meaning. This particular alchemy comes about when we go beyond the surface and address what is of lasting value:

- that a person is not more valuable by virtue of having valuables;

- that a person thinks clearly when they come to the same conclusion despite all others changing their minds, and only adapts their view in light of new facts not new opinions;

- that a person is wealthy in proportion to the things they can let go;

- that a person is happy when living in accordance with their nature, who is unshaken by what happens externally; and

- a person gains a more well-ordered mind when they realize the greatest harms are the ones we inflict upon ourselves.

It is clear that the recipe for a good life is available to all, but preparing it well is not the work of amateurs.

The Irish poet Oscar Wilde had this in mind when he said:

> To live is the rarest thing in the world. Most people exist, that is all.

If you would be accomplished in this effort, I commend to you the words of the Indian lawyer Mahatma Gandhi, who counseled:

> Live as if you were to die tomorrow. Learn as if you were to live forever.

It is the serious student who takes every opportunity to be about their studies.

If you spend your time in reading and contemplation, you will not miss your life by bending to your books but will instead find it.

Be well.

Chapter Ten

On Your New Blog

Acquire new knowledge while thinking over the old, and you may become a teacher of others

I see you have taken my recent words to heart, dear reader, and put your own words to paper in the hope of giving them meaning.

I meant to take a quick look at the new blog that you have started on the side, with the intention of making a thorough study later. But I was drawn in, and I can't say against my will, for I was glad to remain immersed in your thoughts.

When I came back to my senses, I was amazed to see that the afternoon was gone, and the sun had already set. The dog needed walking, the other animals clamored to be fed, and I had missed my office hours that day. Judging from the Post-it notes now coloring the surface of my door, there is no shortage of students looking for guidance who also turned away with their needs unmet today.

Students of the good life could scarcely do better than to consume your writing themselves. It seems another master has entered our midst, and your voice rings out clearly among the greats.

How pleased I am! Not just at your progress, for what teacher does not rejoice at the accomplished student, but that you are breaking new ground and charting new territory. I see in your blog entries what I was trying to describe as the signs of understanding: You are not just reformulating what you have heard but finding new insights.

I am called to mind the words of that great Chinese philosopher Confucius, who said:

> Acquire new knowledge while thinking over the old, and you may become a teacher of others.

I had to share these first impressions at once, but you deserve a studied response. I will give you my thoughts in more detail after they have had time to marinate and mature.

And I promise to be a true friend and tell you no lies. It is sometimes cruel to be kind, and I would not spare you the rod if your course needs correction.

But if I find you have strayed, I will be a little more lenient than Confucius was when he said:

> If I raise one corner for someone and he cannot come back with the other three, I do not go on.

I will grant you the second corner, dear reader, for I wish you to continue on in this way.

When you share genuine insight with others, you learn something of yourself, even as they learn something of you.

Be well.

Chapter Eleven

On Good Examples

The best way to become wealthy is to become rich in your mind. Plunder the wisdom of the ages and take into your ownership your self-possession

We do not lack for knowledge of what to do, we lack the will to do it.

The collective wisdom of humanity lays revealed before us. We need not even leave our homes to browse these volumes, for they are never farther than an internet search away.

Do not give yourself the excuse, dear reader, that you do not know the path when you fail to seek it. Many have gone before you and you need but follow in their footsteps.

For myself, though I may sit alone on a bench with my face to the sun, I am in the presence of many teachers:

- the lessons of Confucius are before my eyes as if I sat in his classroom;

- the words of Cicero ring out as if I was in the forum to

hear them delivered live;

- when I call to mind Seneca's letters to Lucilius, I feel they are written directly to me; and

- though Marcus Aurelius was recording his personal thoughts, it is as though they are playing out in my own head.

No matter where I am and no matter what I am doing, I have these examples always before me.

I can almost see them gathered around me like force ghosts. It helps me to imagine they are watching me just as I am watching them.

In this way, I know not only *what* to do, I feel myself encouraged daily to take the proper steps to *do* what I ought to do.

The only riches you can be guaranteed to possess are those that are contained within you.

External things come and go, and their pursuit will distract you from things that matter.

The best way to become wealthy is to become rich in your mind. Plunder the wisdom of the ages and take into your ownership your self-possession.

When your thoughts have thus become well-ordered by following the good examples of others, then you become a good example yourself, able to pass on your riches to future generations in ways that no inheritance tax can diminish.

Be well.

Chapter Twelve

On Continuing Education

I myself try to be an earnest student. Though I am far removed from my formal school days, I am never far from a book or an idea

I put to you last the burden of constant vigilance, of watching your mind lest it become infected with viruses and weaknesses that would sap your reason. I told you that this daily toil cannot be avoided because the threats to your ordered mind are themselves unceasing and unrelenting.

I have more than just bitter news on offer, dear reader, and today I will give you a message that is sweeter, though it too is about serious things.

Just as people are creatures of habit and we become what we repeatedly do, so your mind becomes more skilled with practice at spotting and blocking the viruses that bombard you. With your daily habit of reflecting upon and reinforcing your reason, you will readily spot traps and dead ends.

This is not to say that you become unthinking and take for granted what you have learned, but that the lessons spring more easily to your mind and to your defense when needed.

But do not rest on your accomplishments, my dear reader, for you are never further than one step from a fall. Our friend Confucius advises us to

> Pursue the study of virtue as though you could never reach your goal, and were afraid of losing the ground already gained

and surely this is sound advice. Even though you may gain confidence in the subjects of your daily meditation, are you confident you have learned everything that may be of use to you?

Let us hear again the voice of Confucius, who made no claim to wisdom for himself, but once more praised the virtue of the student:

> In me, knowledge is not innate. I am but one who loves antiquity, and is earnest in the study of it.

I myself try to be an earnest student. Though I am far removed from my formal school days, I am never far from a book or an idea.

ON CONTINUING EDUCATION

If passions and desires are missiles and bullets being fired constantly at our vulnerable reason, ideas and beliefs are the shields that protect us. I would rather carry a thousand shields about my person than I should find myself missing the one that could have protected me from a cruel blow!

So I suit myself for school as diligently as the parent preparing their child for kindergarten, reflective band about their neck, pack upon their back, and mid-day snack at the ready.

"Look how foolish he is to be marching back to school with the smallest of children," the ignorant will mock. I should be so lucky to always have such feeble-minded critics.

I fully admit to knowing but a fraction of all that I could and all that I would. The criticisms of the empty-headed are more a reflection upon them than upon me. I dismiss them as easily as I do the impatient honking of the commuter at the schoolchildren's crosswalk who is eager to get to their work cell so they do not need to be confronted with the prison they've made of their minds.

Here's something I've realized in my later years that those who are students only in their youth may never learn. The toil seems greater which never varies and is repeated over and over.

Sisyphus could have been made to perform any punishment, but Zeus set him to push a boulder endlessly up a hill. How like Sisyphus are people in their pursuit of money and objects, always the same distance from their goals no matter how far they have come, doomed to struggle without end and without ever nearing satisfaction.

How different the task laid before the willing lifelong student! We have before us a rich buffet of delicacies whose recipes have been created, experimented upon, and improved across ages. This month we are dining on Chinese food, next month it is European fare that best suits our palates, and later we may enjoy the heat and spice of India. Is it a fusion of tastes you are after? No problem, for every combination is available for the taking.

When you are feeling full, by all means, take some time for digestion. Did that last dish not agree with you so much? Put it to the side for now. I wouldn't discard it, even though it is not to my taste, because I remember two things: It appealed to someone in time and it would be interesting to know why; and even if I do not enjoy the meal the first time I try it, perhaps I will find it to be an acquired taste or that it is improved when consumed with other flavors.

We each try many things in our pursuit of happiness and meaning. The usual burdens and cares we pick up as we age make us heavier and wear us down. By contrast, the meals we consume in knowledge and learning make us lighter the more we eat. Let us therefore put work into the task of ordering our minds. If we can stick with this effort, I feel sure we will be rewarded.

For every degree that our perception sharpens, we see that there is more to be seen. For everything that we think we have come to know and understand, we should be looking about in delight because there is so much more that we do not.

The wisest person is the one who is least confident of the extent of their wisdom. To learn, to study, to engage with great minds: This is work but no burden, this is effort but no toil.

If we have compassion for humankind, let us make it our mission to help more people realize that while material things offer meager and fleeting rewards, reason's rewards are abundant.

It seems only proper to let Confucius close for me today dear reader. He has been my faithful companion throughout and can reinforce today's learnings in his own words:

> I used to spend whole days without food and whole nights without sleep, in order to meditate. But I made no progress. Study, I found, was better. It is not easy to find a man who after three years of self-cultivation has not reached happiness.

Be well.

Chapter Thirteen

On the Best Course of Study

If you would not have your children tear down the foundations that hold up society, do not send them into the factories that labor explicitly for that purpose

You want me to tell you the best course of study for a young person, for an older person, or for any person for that matter.

You may expect, as I did when I first applied myself to the task of answering your question, that a clear answer exists.

- For example, the only truly useful course of study is the one that trains the mind to be well-ordered and follow reason.

- That the only sincere students are those who learn to look within and follow the precepts of philosophy.

There is something to this, but I do not think we should be satisfied with a quick answer. Just as the philosopher would, let us look below the surface to see what further insight we can glean.

I would argue that the serpent in the Garden of Eden was the first in a long line of philosophers who used clever logic and sophistry to support a line of argument that leads to conclusions that are either of little use to their students or downright harmful.

In any event, what Adam and Eve gained by eating from the Tree of Knowledge was not wisdom but self-awareness. They became aware of their nakedness and the nature of good and evil.

How bitter that the first human consequence of their newfound awareness was for Adam and Eve to seek to shirk responsibility for their actions: Adam blames his eating the fruit on Eve, and Eve blames her eating the fruit on the serpent.

God curses all three of them. Eve's curse is painful childbirth and subjugation to her husband while Adam is cursed to a lifetime of hard labor followed by death. Thus did the first humans fall and suffer ejection from paradise.

The first children did not fare much better. Cain is jealous that his brother Abel's sacrifices were favored more by God. Cain murders Abel, for which he is condemned to a life of wandering.

"What does any of this have to do with my question?" I can hear you wondering.

Well, dear reader, in my own wandering I am working my way to the first point, which is this: Before setting yourself on the path of seeking knowledge, be aware that knowledge is dangerous. Its acquisition comes with the burdens of awareness and responsibility that cannot simply be laid aside.

One of the most fundamental things humans became aware of is that there are differences between people. Thus, Eve was subject to the rule of Adam, and Cain sees that Abel's sacrifices were better received by God.

From the very beginning, the human ability to reason brought with it the drawing of distinctions between humans. Almost everything we do in our lives, including the courses of study we choose and the attendant careers we put ourselves on the path to pursuing, serves to delineate these distinctions more sharply.

Do you see now why some gurus have retreated from society into their solitary mountain caves? To be among the company of other people is to be constantly reminded of our differences, and for many, like Cain, this is not a source of joy.

And yet, people are intensely social in the sense that most wither and suffer miserably when they are deprived of interaction with their fellow humans. The worst punishment you can inflict on a person is not physical torture but solitary confinement.

So, the hermit's cave is habitable by only a tiny minority and does not offer suitable accommodation for the vast majority of humankind. What to do then? How to organize ourselves so that we can co-exist without literally killing each other by virtue of perceiving differences between ourselves?

With this context in mind, I think you will more readily accept that one of the great purposes of education is to socialize people into getting along. We are seeking foremost to teach conformity to the rules of society because the alternatives are anarchy and warfare.

Culture and acculturation are the aim, from the first day of kindergarten onwards. Though it may be the veneer we use to cover the core mission, the acquisition of knowledge is secondary.

I believe most founders of schools and universities genuinely wanted to better the condition of humankind.

Whether it was their intention from the start to shape generations of students in the mold of useful conformists, this has been the effect. And I do not say this is wrong, dear reader.

For modern society to work at all we need to accept a set of common values and common conditions. Even though much of what we take for granted is quite arbitrary, the common suspension of disbelief is what makes cooperation among competitive, aggressive, and emotional people possible.

Education at every level bends itself to the task of bending minds within lines of acceptable thought and guidelines of acceptable behavior. Conformity of thought is an incredibly powerful tool to shape the culture of society.

And herein lies a great danger. The very tools of education that humankind developed to keep us from each other's throats can also be used to turn society to other purposes.

In the past few decades, we have seen the steady growth and subsequent march of postmodernism across much of higher education.

Postmodernists would tear away the common blinders we have collectively put across our eyes to expose a different underlying reality. Not for the sake of any objective truth but in the naked pursuit of power. To a postmodernist, structures in society

ON THE BEST COURSE OF STUDY

are questions of what ideologies create political and economic power, and who controls those ideologies.

In effect, I have been arguing from the same premise that they do: Our whole system of education is a structure designed to direct society in a desired direction.

The as-yet irreconcilable flaw in all our systems is that we have not been able to eradicate human differences. Without exception, every society we know generates hierarchies and this is by no means limited to the human realm.

In hierarchies, there are winners and losers, the powerful and the weak, the happy and the dissatisfied. Cain is long since dead and gone, but his spirit lives on within each of us. When we detect a difference, murderous envy is never far from the surface, and never so safely hidden that we can relax our guard.

I submit that postmodernists see themselves as the inherently weak and unhappy, the losers under the modern rules of life, at least in their own minds. Surely it must be so, for why else would they propound theories that have as their effect the *complete destruction* of modern society as we currently know it?

Do you think I exaggerate? Consider that the targets of postmodernist criticism include objective reality and truth, human nature and morality, reason, science and social progress, and even language. What sort of society will we have once we have cast all these to the curb?

Make no mistake: We are in a battle for the future of human society, for the very soul of humankind.

By assuming that schools and universities are doing today what they did a century ago, we have let loose predators amongst our children. We are surprised to see our children turn into predators themselves, tearing at the very throat of society on what seems to be the slightest provocation. Is the answer to a perceived unfairness to tear everything down?

As we look upon the rubble in shock, I say we should not waste time in trying to lay blame, as in "Why didn't we see this sooner? Why wasn't anyone paying attention?" The damage is done, and the question now is one of survival.

Thus, I come at last to the first answer to your question on the best course of study for those of all ages: It is not to be found in any modern school or university. Worse, by subjecting yourself to their ministrations, you risk making yourself a tool in the destruction of society. Would you be an unwitting soldier in this army?

Now I am not advocating that we remain ignorant, nor that we remove ourselves from the fight. The fight is coming to the willing and unwilling alike. Your only choice is the manner in which you will enter the battle.

Do you send your own children to be warriors for the enemy? If you would not have them tear down the foundations that hold up society, do not send them into the factories that labor explicitly for that purpose.

"Do you really mean to suggest that we must home-school our children?" you ask, "Not everyone has the luxuries of time or money to do this, and what does the average person know of teaching all that is necessary for modern life?"

These are the wrong questions, dear reader, and I despair that people will open their eyes in time to see. There is something worse than trying one's best and doing a poor job, and that is others trying their best to do an evil thing.

- Is it better that you leave your car sitting un-serviced in your driveway or that you take it to a mechanic you know will pour salt in the tank and cut the wires?

- Are you not wiser to take your health into your own hands than to visit the doctor who will prescribe you poison?

Our salvation lies in independence of thought and action because this is incredibly dangerous to the stability of an ideology.

This is why the mob reacts so strongly to having its orthodoxy challenged. Cancel culture is nothing more than the impulse to destroy what is deemed to be an attack on the desired view.

For almost all of humanity, I would have said conformity to the mainstream view was the safest course. But when the current view is that society shall be destroyed, our only course is to reclaim the moral high ground by refusing to submit.

Thus, the best course of study is to see first to your own education and then that of others.

Be well.

Chapter Fourteen

On How To Study Philosophy

Philosophy means the love of wisdom and consequently is made up of the efforts you put into attaining wisdom

So, having urged you to be about your own studies, can I be surprised when you ask me for guidance about how and in in what direction?

No, although I urged you not to put your mind in the care of those who would weaponize you for their own purposes, I would have you weaponize your mind in defense of yourself. And I suppose you will not be surprised when I tell you that the lessons you need to learn most ardently are those of philosophy.

I have previously urged you to read broadly and widely. This is because you do not know where and how inspiration will strike. It comes to people unevenly and at different times, and what works for one may be useless for another.

The best way to increase your chances of success, at least initially, is to make many tries at the prize. If one lottery ticket gives you but a tiny chance, then a hundred or a thousand tickets will multiply your odds.

But your odds will remain forever slight if you do not lay a certain groundwork; otherwise, your reading will be aimless and fruitless, like buying lottery tickets for last week's drawing.

Wisdom is what you are seeking, my dear reader, the highest attainment of the well-ordered mind in pursuit of reason. Philosophy means the love of wisdom and consequently is made up of the efforts you put into attaining wisdom.

I have talked with you many times about virtues and vices, about first- and second-order goods or pursuits, and about the many things that lead people astray from the path of reason. Although these distinctions give rise to much confusion, what is clear is that philosophers are on a path seeking wisdom through philosophy.

Philosophy does not follow a single path but offers multiple branches.

- We talk of moral philosophy, which is concerned with the thinking, motivation, and actions of people.

- Natural philosophy takes up our observations of the universe we find ourselves in and everything in it. In the meantime, this branch has diverged into the many roads that lead to the hard sciences.

- Finally, we have logical philosophy, which addresses how humans make sense of the universe through words and expressions, and how to build logical

ON HOW TO STUDY PHILOSOPHY

arguments from unbroken chains of reasoning. We most often turn to logical philosophy to identify falsehoods, for these are more abundant and easier to identify than eternal truths.

I urge you to build your foundation in moral philosophy, and within it to focus on the most critical question of how to discern what is truly valuable and all the things that are not.

Your motives are only partly under your control and will steer you to wrong action if left unchecked, but they can be brought under the domain of reason. For you to apply right reason at all you need to know what is worth pursuing.

I repeat myself to you often, dear reader, because these basic lessons bear repeating. Without this clear understanding of the relative value of things, all else you pursue will be to false purposes and likely wasted effort.

- You should understand that bravery is one of the ways to overcome fear, but that fear itself is a construct of the mind.

- You should know the value and correct application of loyalty, temperance, and kindness.

- You will never waste your time if you are spending it studying how to live your life simply, modestly, and with self-restraint.

Although knowledge of the things that are valuable is the cornerstone on which your good life will be built, your tower will not raise itself towards the sky unaided. You create the structure of your life by taking actions consistent with your values.

Each time you act unthinkingly, you have missed an opportunity to lift a stone and cement it into place. Each time you act inconsistently, you are a sloppy builder, sometimes creating a smooth surface by accident but more often leaving sharp edges that you will need to return to later for repair.

And if you act against your values, you are tearing down your substance and creating destruction around you, though at first, you may be the only one to sense it.

Do you feel that I am preaching to you again, dear reader? I know the only one whose words will have lasting effect are your own, so I call upon you to be your own constant cheerleader if not a stern policeman.

Until you bring your thinking into order and direct your actions consistently with your thinking, you will have to resign yourself to my lessons. I will not stop talking until you have put a stop to your desires, for it is your desires that lead you from the path every time.

Once you can test your wishes and reliably return the answer that you have enough, so will my words cease — you will have had enough of them because they are ingrained in your being.

In sum, you study not to learn more things but to learn what things are valuable.

You think about what you have studied to prepare yourself to apply the learnings to your particular situation. And though no exam is administered in this course, still you test yourself in every situation where you are called upon to make a choice about how to act and how to feel about your actions.

You will know you are making progress in your studies if the wise decision is clear to you, even though it still costs you constant vigilance to control your motivation and constant effort to control your actions. This is enough to be on the path to wisdom and headed in the right direction.

Be well.

Chapter Fifteen

On Precepts (Sayings)

The next best thing to having good examples by your side is to have precepts never far from mind

You know that I have at times made comments critical of psychology. I should be as critical in my comments on philosophy, dear reader, for the root cause of the problem in both cases is the nature of people.

In both fields, our mistakes in both theory and practice come from assuming that two people in the same situation will behave in the same way, or that even a single person will act similarly when the same situation is repeated.

Psychology at least has gained popular attention and broad appeal while Stoic philosophy remains the dusty preserve of the solitary academic.

Why the difference? Both are after all concerned with the workings of the mind and with understanding the motivations behind our actions. They spring from the same deep-seated sense of wondering, "If only we could understand why we do what we do, could we find a way to be enduringly happy?"

If we begin with similar topics and we pursue similar aims, the conclusions of the two fields and our corresponding prescriptions to adherents surely differ. Psychology tells us that nothing is our fault, while philosophy tells us that everything is.

The psychologist will say that we are creatures formed as a result of our environments, starting with our childhood experiences and traumas and continuing on through to the inputs and stimuli we receive every day.

- The path to happiness lies in first making sense of our pasts and then in carefully controlling our environments to ensure we are confronted only with surroundings that lift us up.

- At a minimum, we shall avoid people and situations that bring us down.

The philosopher says that we are creatures formed by our minds and that the path to happiness lies in ordering our minds to follow reason in any environment.

- People should not seek to control their circumstances but to control their thinking about circumstances.

- We do not flee from hardship. Rather we see that overcoming hard times can be more beneficial to wellbeing than being surrounded with ease and luxury.

Is it any wonder that philosophy molders while psychology thrives?

ON PRECEPTS (SAYINGS)

Which doctors are more eagerly greeted by their patients? The ones who say sternly "You need to make some serious lifestyle changes because the path you're heading down is going to lead to inevitable sadness, sickness, and decay."

Or the ones who whip out their prescription pads with a smile, saying "Good news! You currently show signs of A, B, and C, and in a few years left untreated, you will almost certainly develop X and Y. But I can prescribe you this small army of pills, taken twice daily with meals, and you'll be right as rain."

Do you doubt that most people would rather take a pill that merely conceals their symptoms than undertake a course of treatment that will result in a lasting cure but only if they put in serious effort?

I say for all their wisdom, philosophers have fundamentally misunderstood human nature if they think their bitter medicine will be easily swallowed.

Is this the reason that sayings and precepts are in such widespread use when we talk of philosophy to the masses?

- If our whole treatment is too much for the patient to take at one time, perhaps we can dole out our medicine in bite-sized pieces.

- Taken individually, the maxims of philosophy are lighter fare, and easier to consume, remember, and repeat.

And so now we come to the question of whether these treatments are any real help against the underlying maladies humankind suffers from, or whether we too are quacks purveying snake oil to unwitting rubes at the country fair.

When we dispense philosophical precepts, do we only smooth over symptoms and leave our mortally ill patients not only uncured but unaware that they are still terminal?

We can approach our answer from two sides, top-down and bottom-up.

Starting first from the lofty heights of the philosopher who has achieved wisdom.

- This person knows that reason is the only virtue and that following the judgment of their well-ordered mind is the path to happiness.

- Such a person has no need for maxims because they need but consult their reason to know the true value of all things in every situation.

- Their course of action is not prescribed by others because they are the physician of their own soul at all times.

The point of sayings is not to cure the philosopher who has attained reason, but to help raise up all others who are not yet safely underway.

Let us therefore consider the situation from the bottom up, from the perspective of the condition we all find ourselves in much of the time, which is that of needing help.

To one who needs help seeing, to say nothing of acting, does a simple saying provide valuable guidance by lighting the way?

I assume for our discussion, dear reader, that our patients are desirous of seeing their way out of suffering and troubles. I say this knowing all too well that there are none so blind as those who do not want to see. But for the willfully blind neither precept, nor theory, nor practice in any discipline will bear lasting fruit. So, I limit myself to the case of the willing student with an attentive ear.

For such students, sayings are a sweet starter that whets the appetite. Not fully satisfying in themselves but providing encouragement to consume more.

We should all be encouraged to think about useful topics and be given a helpful nudge in the right direction. The hardest part of many tasks is to start, and if the saying prompts us into motion, then it has already served a useful purpose.

Once started, we benefit from support along the way. Give me a tip on how to improve my running form while I am running, and I am delighted to hear it. Tell me how to conserve energy, improve my endurance, stand straighter, step quicker — there is no end to the advice on many small things that I will gladly take on if I have the slightest sense it will help me in my current pursuit.

Though neither a new running shoe with a carbon sole, nor a T-shirt with sweat-wicking fabric, nor a new electrolyte drink will make me into a champion by themselves, they each give me a helpful push to continue. And if that push is only in my mind, but prompts me to start, then is that not where the proper motivation to undertake any great deed ultimately begins?

A saying will not do the hard work for you. It can only offer support.

But though sayings are not complete, and we ourselves have to lift and put one foot in front of the other, who does not welcome support at every stage? Whether you're just starting out, or nearing the finish line, you still appreciate the clapping and calls of encouragement during the race.

It is no doubt most beneficial to have good examples in the form of other people, personal teachers as it were, to show us the way.

The next best thing to having good examples by your side is to have precepts never far from mind. These are the written condensation of the best examples of people across time.

We no longer have access to Plato and Socrates or to the painted porch of the Stoics, but we have access to their sayings. If it helps you to think on the wisdom behind the words, then imagine someone saying them aloud to you, and having a conversation with them in your head.

Learning to follow reason more often than emotion is a race we must run slowly and steadily. I always say that it is not your speed that matters but simply that you continue to progress. Your steps will fall more lightly the more you practice.

The more you are reminded to practice, for example by keeping a saying close to hand, the more you reinforce and stay your course.

Will a life lived purely by sayings result in your becoming wise in all things? Or is more required, for example, the study of doctrines, or theories, underlying our philosophy? I will take up this topic another time.

For now, I want to sound a note of caution in case I have made the path to progress sound easy to find and trivial to maintain.

Look around, dear reader, and ask yourself how comfortable you feel that humankind is safely out of range from the barbarism we have descended to over and over throughout history. Take these words of Seneca from 2,000 years ago, and ask if he could not have been writing today:

> There are many who set fire to cities ... no one withstood their attack; but they themselves could not withstand desire for power and the impulse to cruelty; at the time when they seemed to be hounding others, they were themselves hounded. Do you believe that the man was in his senses who could begin by devasting Greece, the land where he received his education?

Replace "Greece" with "the United States" and you have your description of modern critical theory, Antifa, BLM, and anti-Zionists.

When Seneca reminds us that the path to happiness is never found in making others unhappy, he admonishes us to heal ourselves before looking to change the world.

When we are surrounded by burning and chaos, we should avoid the flames and consume the good advice that philosophy so abundantly offers in the form of sayings.

Be well.

Chapter Sixteen

On a Learning Mind

When you are told by experts what to think you may become a believer, but you will not become a thinker

Have you ever considered what makes for a successful student, dear reader? I am talking now about a traditional college or university student of any subject, and not just the study of philosophy.

Back when people were interested in at least predicting such things, to say nothing of understanding them, they devised a method in the form of the standardized test.

The very names behind the tests' abbreviations reveal their erstwhile purpose: Scholastic Aptitude Test and American College Testing. Each year aspiring high school students across the U.S. would sit down to the SAT or ACT exams and seek to demonstrate that they had sufficient understanding of reading, writing, math, and reasoning to succeed in higher education.

Admissions officers gave great weight to standardized test scores because they were highly correlated to students' ability to successfully complete a traditional university education. More than any transcript of impressive-looking grades or carefully concocted but unrepresentative essays, for almost a hundred years the SAT provided a stark, objective assessment of your relative readiness.

"You are writing about standardized testing in the past tense," you observe. "Aren't the tests still administered and used in college admissions?"

Though our college days are behind us, they are indelibly etched in memory. You would be wrong to think, dear reader, that your college experience shares anything beyond the name with what students today experience.

More than 900 institutions of higher learning had already made the switch to so-called "test-optional" admissions prior to the pandemic. COVID-19 gave an excuse for many of the remaining universities, including all the Ivy League and many of the top liberal arts colleges, to drop the SAT/ACT testing requirement.

What has driven this rapid and widespread change? Aren't universities still interested in knowing which students are prepared for the rigors of higher education?

I have told you before that divining motivation is not easy, but we can default to observing actions and inferring intentions along the way. Let us look at the actions of the players involved in university education and see what inferences we may draw.

"What players do you mean," you ask.

I am thinking of universities themselves, including their professors and administrators; the people paying for the cost of education; and the prospective students themselves.

Consider first the university ecosystem, which I consider to be a professional machine. Having spent years toiling in professional service firms of lawyers, and decades more employing them alongside accountants, tax specialists, bankers, and others, believe me when I tell you I can recognize some of the features of the professional model.

At the very top, you have the owners or equity partners, to whom residual profits flow. They number the least and earn the most. Naturally, competition is fierce to become a full partner, or in the case of the university, a tenured professor.

The partner/professor is supported directly by an army of striving hopefuls, let us call them associates or adjunct professors. The leverage ratio differs from setting to setting, but the common feature is that there are many more people seeking promotion than will ultimately be elevated.

Whether it is 10–1, 7–1, or some other number is irrelevant. What matters is that the competition for advancement is fierce.

As a result, the associate/adjunct is the modern equivalent of the Roman slave, theoretically on a path to purchasing their freedom but until then toiling away for little more than their daily ration of bread and water.

Do they teach the classics with joy in their hearts? No, the bitterness of envy, the despair of fighting the system, and the anger at the unfairness of it all, oozes forth from their lessons, though you will find them nowhere on the syllabus.

The self-destructiveness of critical theory, defining every relationship in terms of relative power, springs directly from the bent backs and bent minds of failed academics.

- If material success is found in the world of business,

then the businessperson must be achieving their success by oppressing others who are weaker.

- If one group has enjoyed more successful outcomes in life, it must be because they have taken advantage of others who are further down on the ladder.

How can these adjuncts and professors think otherwise, when the evidence is all around them?

If the university environment has grown petty with such poisonous thoughts, what explains the growth in university admissions? What student would willingly thrust themselves into this maw of pity and self-hate?

Well, the message that the world is an unforgiving, competitive place begins long before college, dear reader. From the moment of one's birth society sends you signals, first through your parents but soon enough directly.

"More wealth and possessions are the way to go. You want to be successful and wealthy, don't you? You need a college degree to make it in the world, now more than ever."

Children take on ideology all too readily, for it is their nature to be impressionable. They make the best recruits for armies because they are the easiest to brainwash.

So, the question becomes not whether to go to college, but which college, and how do I get into the "best" one I can?

Universities have done a masterful job of creating perceived scarcity — that is, they are selling something hard to get, when in fact the opposite is true. The credit for this grand marketing job goes to the university administrator.

Though the administrator is a bureaucrat, as far removed from the molding of fresh minds as the cook staff in the cafeteria, they are so much more valuable than even the teachers.

"Why is this," you ask.

Because they feed the machine with new recruits and keep the money flowing. At many universities, the number of administrators has grown to equal or exceed the number of tenured professors. Where once we considered the number of students per class to be indicative of the quality of teaching, we now ask how many support staff there are to grease the wheels of the university machine.

This flow of money is our chance to finally understand what has happened to universities, and why they have so readily jettisoned testing.

When a bank is exposed to the credit risk of their debtor, they will carefully scrutinize the business plan and ability to repay. When a lender carries no risk because the loan is guaranteed, the business model shifts completely. Now the concern is not creditworthiness, but volume.

In the interests of promoting higher education for more Americans, the Federal government guarantees student loans.

The incentives for universities are clear: More loans, in greater amounts, drive greater profits. In just the last fifteen years, the amount of student loan debt in the U.S. has more than *tripled* to over $1.7 trillion.

Now do you see why standardized testing had to go, with its nasty suggestion that some students were more suited for higher learning than others? Is it now much easier to understand why universities seem to care little anymore for imparting knowledge but spread only spite and social envy?

Do the otherwise lavish expenditures on five-star dining, world-class sports arenas, and soft-pillowed safe spaces now make sense? When the learning itself was once the ultimate measure of a university's worth, can we be surprised that it has now become an afterthought?

"This is so short-sighted," you say. "And it is unsustainable. Don't universities see that they are sowing the seeds of their own destruction? That at most in one or two generations, the students so ill-treated will wreak ruin on society?"

At their most fundamental, dear reader, I believe humans are good at learning short-term lessons and poor at divining long-term consequences.

A short-term incentive to make money will outweigh long-term risks every time. The business cycle of boom and bust would not otherwise exist and persist as it does. Despite the wracking financial crises we let loose every 10 to 20 years like clockwork, the next generation either never learned or self-servedly forgets the lessons of the previous generation.

At last, we come to the students themselves and the conditions for a learning mind.

A successful student is least likely to be nurtured where dogma exists, by which I mean unquestioned acceptance of conventional wisdom. When you are told by experts what to think you may become a believer, but you will not become a thinker.

The reaction of many youths has been to simply ignore the voices of their elders because they have rightly perceived their elders are no wiser about so many things.

But from this promising start, many youths have drawn a terribly mistaken conclusion: That they already know everything they need to know about themselves and about how the world works.

I tell you the only successful student is one who keeps a learning and open mind. That sounds like a definition by definition, but what I mean is this: If you are convinced you know everything, you cannot learn anything.

- If you do not question, you will not learn.
- If you do not doubt, you will not progress.
- If you do not listen, you will not hear. You do not need to listen uncritically, but you do need to listen.

And as you are listening, you will need to develop the second condition of the learning mind. This is to learn to live with uncertainty and doubt.

Some of your cherished ideas will be challenged! You may be wrong about things you felt strongly about. You may discover that some things you took as fact were just narrative. That the narratives you have been fed since birth have been created to serve purposes that may not serve your purposes.

Upon deeper reflection, you may find nuance and perspective that your youthful ideology was entirely unaware of.

It is in the times of greatest uncertainty and doubt that the learning mind makes the greatest progress. You will not find this progress in a safe space.

Allow yourself to become uncomfortable so that you may become learned, and you will be on the path to wisdom.

Be well.

Chapter Seventeen

On New Students

Philosophy always welcomes new students

I am happy to hear that your conversation with the wealthy and now questioning parent has gone well. It is usually all but impossible to be objectively heard when discussing how someone is raising their children.

It is a testament to your powers of persuasion that you managed to get them past the point of doubt to the desire for a change. Philosophy always welcomes new students, and we hope this parent is taking the first steps on the path to wisdom.

The desire for change is certainly a necessary precondition for progress. But it is just as certainly insufficient to carry the new student far.

Your friend comes to you in a desperate state because they have been too successful in life.

"Too successful? What do you mean? Should their proven track record at overcoming obstacles not also help them pursue a different path now?"

You have only temporarily caused your friend to question the wisdom of their choices, dear reader. Consider the forces arrayed against your further progress: Their family, their other friends, and all of society.

Then there is their own mind, which we know is an unreliable partner unless honed by the most rigorous of training. They will think back on all they have done; all they have accomplished. In their old life, they were the master, the unquestioned conqueror. Now they are the novice, starting all over from the bottom of the hill.

No doubt your friend means well. You have flamed the nagging discontent into a discomfort they no longer feel they can ignore. But if it was an excess of luxury that brought them to this pass, they will also be sorely tempted to let their past luxuries lull them back into submission.

After a break from fine things, they will find their entreaties all the more alluring. They presently think they cannot live with their vices, but they will soon realize they cannot live without them.

By all means, encourage your student to continue, and be a role model as much as you are an active teacher. But let's see for how long their actions match their resolve before we welcome a new pilgrim in our midst.

Be well.

Made in the USA
Monee, IL
03 May 2026